Random
REFLECTIONS

JAN O'LEARY

Random REFLECTIONS

MEMOIRS
Cirencester

Published by Memoirs

MEMOIRS
PUBLISHING

1A The Wool Market, Dyer Street, Cirencester, Gloucestershire, GL7 2PR
info@memoirsbooks.co.uk www.memoirspublishing.com

Random reflections

ISBN: 978-1-86151-157-7

INTRODUCTION

In June 2012 I was admitted to hospital for a simple hip replacement. Unfortunately I sustained a perioperative complication of a cervical cord infarct, a rare condition which caused paralysis of my right arm and both lower limbs.
I have slowly regained some movement in my arm and one leg. Meanwhile my iPad has been my life line; it has kept my mind alive while my limbs have lain dormant.
With time on my hands I started jotting down my random thoughts. The rhyming couplets occurred by chance.

DEDICATION

With loving appreciation to my carers, especially my primary one, who has supported me in his ninetieth year, not the time of life to learn new skills. He deserves a fifth gallantry medal!
Thank you to our family for their time given so generously helping us with the challenge of the ageing process.

My thanks to Chris Newton and Tony Tingle at Memoirs Books for putting these poems into print.

FOREST SANCTUARY

Concealed behind the rows of pine
In a forest is a special church I call mine.
It's near where I saw my children grow
It's neglected and forsaken now.
The years when we frequented it
The brass shining and the candles lit
Linen gleaming white and stiffly starched
Down the aisle a blue carpet marched.
The pews were shining polished oak
The congregation country folk.

I arranged many flowers on a stand
To welcome those who had come to attend
As they came through the heavy main door
And crossed over the tiled mosaic floor.
They entered beneath a Madonna and babe
Situated high with Her marble robe,
Watching over us as we prayed
Were baptised, married and dispatched.
The church was small, sitting only a few
If plump, then only four to a pew.
Led by an American Franciscan priest
Living there alone, he became our guest
When tragedy struck the presbytery
And his housekeeper met her destiny.

Fate decreed her time had come, a fire
In the kitchen made the room a pyre.
Sadly Ivy needed her inhaler, but her heart
Decided it was time for her to depart.
Another chapter in the church's life
Commenced on that day of grief and strife.

The Bishop decided to separate the building
And up for auction went the priest's dwelling
We did not listen to our hearts which said
Buy me and preserve the statues and lead
On the roof of the church by being on guard.
The decision not to bid was very hard
So the new owner had a pack of huskies
Which frightened the lives of the attendees
At Mass, when the cries of wolves gave forth
And all were filled with trepidation and wrath.

The sanctuary where I meditated changed
People melted away, numbers decreased
As the priest lived miles away in a town
Sadly the seeds of doubt were sown.
It did not help when we also relocated
After, in retirement, we contemplated
Whether to try and gently rejuvenate
This special place where we congregate.
And we regret not keeping a candle alight
Shining warmly in the forest day and night.

DOCTORS

If I could have my life again
With new options in which to train
I would like to study to be
A useful member of society
Perhaps to cure as well as care
In nursing I would have liked to share
A doctor's skilled expertise
A physician, to diagnose disease.
From signs able to identify
The pointers which signify
That not all is quite right
Within a doctor's sight.
Or the symptoms which suggest
That the patient does know best
When they complain of pain
Nature's way to explain
That not all is well
It is a good way to tell.
One has to listen with ears and eyes
As a detective, investigate cries
For help, from a suffering person
Before the conditions worsen.
Then when treatment is pursued
And perhaps reluctantly endured
Because of what you discover,
The patient may finally recover.

LOSS OF INDEPENDENCE

When you are off your feet
And admit to defeat
You need help and care
Days long gone for an au pair.
So you weigh up your needs
Then count up the deeds
Juggle all the pounds
Will they do the rounds?
Should we have a late
Meal, prepared on a plate
In the morning or lunch?
Compromise, have brunch
I must remember to pee
When a carer I see
Not be left high and dry
And ready to cry

But be an opportunist
Not a contortionist.
Life's a challenge to see
What can be done for a fee.
The agent acts as if it's a favour
To oblige with a carer enabler
I wonder who is paying who
Or if we are last in the queue?
However, the carer is excellent
Very caring and compassionate
I count our blessings and enjoy
Being able to pay to employ
Someone to help in our need
Who does it for a good deed
And not as profit in the bank
For her I have a lot to thank!

LETTING GO

The first week of October now lost for another year,
The memories though linger, sometimes with a silent tear
Reflecting the has been and what could have been.
Pleasures lost of being out in the sun, of which I was keen.
Is this another joy, which I must reluctantly forgo
To explore the flower beds and pots which aren't too low?
Of feeling the healing rays caress my limbs and face
Months ago I believed with effort I was winning this race.
And then a step forward and then two steps back.

Rising from my bed, getting dressed, there is now a lack
Of incentive and for to please those who have tried
With their kindness to persuade me, cajole, help and guide.
How can I betray the care given for over one year
And let all the effort, equipment and energy now disappear?
Time spent with me if I now say enough is enough
I must not refuse to give in because the going gets tough.
I'll rise to the challenge, even faced with adversity
There is still much to do, say and write with skill and diversity.
This iPad for one thing, has kept me enthralled
Spending many hours through the Internet where I've trawled.
I scribble some notes, fingers glued to the screen.
Becoming addicted to the power of words and many a dream
Of years spent in the East, the sights, the smell
Before they fade and escape far away into the past, I'll dwell
On what can be remembered about all the days
Which have been happy, exciting and not too far away.

KITES

Have you ever seen a kite soar high
Weaving and gliding in leaps so spry?
Triangular, box or bird copied in shape
Their antics of darting from the tapes
Which control them tight until a gust
Of wind tears them away and oh! just
Manages to set them, alas quite free.
Away they go on a remarkable spree.
They disappear out of everyone's sight
Trying to follow them is a sad plight.
Miles go by, the earth below one's feet
Vanishes as you run, trying to meet
The elusive escapee which finds a tree
Which it means to embrace and be free.
Now caught up in branches, to its cost
It's sad that its bid for freedom is lost.

QUALITY OVER QUANTITY

Is it debatable to decide
Which is right for the ride?
A short, sharp trot
Before one rots
Or a long gentle hack
Before you hit the sack?
Is it preferable to be
Old and grey
And not rusting away
But with no memory
To recall a name
Ever again?
Or be like a hanging gate
Off its hinges, a debate
When it won't open
Or close?
Is it better to take it away
Or give it a try on a day
When not in a hurry?
A quandary.
I think now that I've tried
Quantity that's supplied
Next time around
I will be bound
To choose quality first
Unless again I am cursed
To remain here until
I'm over the hill!

THE WAITING GAME

Now there is nowhere to venture yet
Maybe later when I've finished this set
Not of tennis or of a bagatelle
But a long life for a spell
Sitting or lying for the passage of time
Wasting the days away seems a crime
But the legs are now very weak
The bones begin to creak.

With the aid of a carer, a Pallas stand
I can lift off my bed try to lend a hand
From my alternative transport
I can see what I've bought.
Ordering on line can be ok if unseen
But it's possible it won't be a dream.

I venture outside down the paths
But I am no good at maths
The plugs are really small and weedy
I thought they were bigger, not seedy
To try their luck planted in a bed
But inches aren't as I said,
They're centimetres and very small
Not what I thought I ordered at all.
I hope I'm around next year
To see if any appear!

INK STAINS

I've seen them in very surprising places
Ankles, knees and even on faces
Mostly black but some cases
Have been decorated roses
That have trailing leaves
Undercover of sleeves
Hiding down cleavages
And back passages
A few out of sight
But none look right
Of skulls and wolves
Is this to scare off fools
Who do not know that the ink
Is to just make you blink and think
For one minute, that the very ugly mark ,
Makes your bite far worse than your bark?

REALLY LETTING GO!

When most of one's life

As nurse, mother and wife

Has always been spent at their call

Come spring, summer, autumn and fall

When no longer in a state to be usefully able

And one of the family, especially a spouse is unable

To fend for himself because he's feeling under the weather

It's the most frustrating sensation not being able to lift even
a feather

That's a slight exaggeration, it's only my lower limbs which
are useless

So to add to my woe, they have become my foe , I cannot
ease the stress

And care for my husband and see to his needs, give in and
concede to others

The pleasure and let him enjoy tender, loving care from
substitute mothers.

BE PREPARED

I have always been a tidy young fledgling, and
not a fussy old hoarder

My large filing cabinet has neat, tidy files in
spick and span order

They are labelled with white labels and black ink,
of course

In alphabetical range, and identifying the source

Of the contents therein, hopefully complete

Up to date which all expectations meet

When searching through my drawers

Nobody should find any flaws.

When looking for will papers

They find lots of tapers

Are they to light a fire?

Surely not a briar

But cremate

It's fate!

HIDDEN STRENGTHS

When strength of mind can be stronger
Than muscles of limbs and heart for longer
If age takes the power away from the arms
And the legs are weaker but the mind is calm.
Clear thinking will achieve the best results
Pursuing and overcoming obstacles and faults.
One takes up the baton and runs in the relay
If not physically but mentally come what may
The hurdles will be taken in turn and cleared
Each day a new challenge, not one to be feared
There are always answers to resolve concern
If you seek and know where to ask and learn.
Not to be proud and scared of losing control
There are always kind people who have a soul
And come into our lives when most required
I am sure by our guardian angels inspired.

GUARDIAN ANGELS

When I feel a slight breeze caress my cheek
There is no need for the visitor to speak
I won't recognise the tone, the eyes or hair
But I will know that a presence is there
I cannot see, feel or hear, I'm just aware
That I am not alone but in loving care.
We all have a guide or perhaps a pair
Who watch over us, come to share
Troubles when the going is rough
And you feel you've had enough
Wait for that comforting ease
It will never fail and cease
To surround and be near
That is love, never fear.

JOB SATISFACTION

I've read somewhere about all the so-called chores
That nurses remember, which has made me pause
To consider, did I too feel that way even for a day?
But I liked my duties, enjoyed the challenge of dirt
Of damp-dusting lockers, beds and all without hurt.
It was lifting which damaged my lower back
No hoists or stand aids or other useful tack
To help me sustain a healthy posture upright
Lifting alone, in the home, with all my might
On the district when business was so brisk
One learnt to cope and wrongly take a risk
Other nursing tasks of giving injections
Without contamination or any infections
Cleaning and hopefully healing leg ulcers
Taking temperatures, feeling pulses
Watching chests heave up and down
Noticing the signs of pain if a frown
Checking pressure areas on the heels
Making sure patients are having meals
Not becoming dehydrated with thirst
Generally, being observant first
And listen and communicate
Never hurry but gently wait
For the patient to tell you
What they want you to do!

TWEENAGERS

We take our health for granted

When young, in our mind is implanted

That we will never become frail and ill

Never become pregnant, but take the pill

Our lives are tidy, everything in order

But look under the beds, we are great hoarders

Of dirty plates, crisp packets and chocolate papers

Some bought for the weekend, used, but for the wrappers.

Take-away pizza half eaten, a coke bottle
or something stronger

An odd sock, a spare smelly trainer, hair gel
and a school blazer.

Girls and boys are the same, quite wild
but think themselves tame

Obsessed with electronic gadgets, iPods, iPads and
war games

A few girly magazines, posters never pinned up as
they were lost

All these bought with paper-round earnings,
never mind the cost

There will be next day, next week, next month
and another year

To face our demons, tidy up rooms and act like a grown up,
our biggest fear!

COACH TRIPS

It's market day, not the easiest time to park
But the coach arrives and makes its mark
Big enough to dominate on the main road
It ignores the demands of the Highway Code
For double yellow lines painted on the side.
And stops to eject all that come for a ride.
Out they slowly alight, a hand on their stick
They are hindered by dodgy hips to be quick.
White cardigans, umbrellas and comfy shoes
Flat caps on the men who are off for a booze.
Their wives in twos propping up one another
Find the tearoom, the one with the pot will be mother
Pouring it out, some strong, no milk, very weak
They all have their likes and sugar cubes sneak.
The diabetics the worst, but just one fruit scone
Won't harm and with cream, jam, time for a moan.
Well it's a special day out, they come once a year
From the over-sixties club with lots of good cheer
They donned their glad rags, hairdos in fine order
From the next county, risk coming over the border
It will be fish, chips and mushy peas for their lunch
And trust their dentures will survive a nice munch.
They will be tired by the time they're ready to leave
But they'll be here again next year, or so they believe.

GRANDCHILDREN

They've arrived through the years until we have nine,
or is it ten?
One is a child of the eldest, so that's one great
grandson and then
Who knows how many more there will be in
another ten years
Bringing much laughter, joy and pleasure, with a few tears
Seeing them develop into fine upright young girls and boys
Some of them now adults enjoying their lives without toys
Venturing out into the great unknown, searching fulfilment
In a career they believe in and can use discernment.
Who knows what lies ahead, what destiny awaits them
A world changing and some injustice they'll condemn.
They will challenge what they see is wrong and not right
Their sense of honour and integrity will give them insight
What more could a grandparent wish them to have?
Not riches, possessions or the fame which some crave
Material things are merely transitory pleasures,
Peace and tranquillity are the genuine treasures!

EXPENSIVE HOBBY

After a really hectic working life
Can you believe my retirement caused strife?
I was bored and did not know what to do
Should I paint, dance, knit, crochet or sew
Or learn French, Mandarin, Latin or Spanish
Yoga, pilates, rest on my laurels and languish?
Something different suddenly appeared
The end of a village shop lease neared
Could I be Arkwright, perhaps not so tight
With money in the till, from dawn to last light
As in 'Open All Hours' on the box? I could sell.
I'd been a district nurse like Gladys Emmanuel.
The two-year lease contract was signed
'Merry Go Round' was painted on the blind.
I was off to a start selling toys made of wood
Beautifully carved, turned and they should
Hopefully bring me a profit if they caught on
The traditional tops and whips going for a song
Dolls and their houses, pull-alongs and hoops
Toy soldiers and bands marching along in troops.
Rocking horses so grand with manes and tails
Enticing young and old to ride, never fails.
The stock paid for from my superannuation
Oh! Why did not I just enjoy a long vacation?

YORK

If there is a place to call home, of York I would talk
A city residing in the far north with very tall
Roman walls surrounding it on which to slowly walk
And look down over the tall grey stone wall
In spring, the grassy embankment covered in flowers
Wordsworth's yellow daffodils for all to see
But dwarfed by the majestic minster's rising towers
Standing there since before seven hundred AD
A proud symbol of human faith in an everlasting life
Witnessing through the years kings come and go
Years of peace, tranquillity and years of warring strife.
The river Ouse rose one year from down below
Flooded many listed buildings, built through the ages.
If you go into the Minster you may find a mouse
Climbing up a lectern, across a pew, under book pages
In the choir carved from oak, not as your house.
Over the south transept is a stained glass rose window
A chequered history, lightning struck the roof
Now restored to all its glory by modern technology, so
Beautiful reflecting light, glass renewed, proof
Of the skill of man, the ability to reclaim what was lost.
York, a city of so many interesting walks to wend
Your way and spend some time to visit, worth the cost
To explore museums, and Dick Turpin met his end.
The smell of chocolate fills the air and Betty's smart cafe
Is waiting to feed and fuel you enough to explore
Petergate, Swinegate, Micklegate and Bootham Bar, it's safe
To say you will enjoy them, plus the Shambles and more.

AFTERNOON TEA

Of all the meals we consume and drink
There's no doubt in my mind, I think
That afternoon tea, especially for me
Is the most elegant and refreshing tea.
Served in porcelain and pretty cups
The handle genteelly held while one sups
With little finger outstretched on high
It's enough to make one give a big sigh
Of content, Darjeeling, Assam or China
There is nothing at all to drink any finer.
Sandwiches thin, crusts cut off the bread
No margarine, only butter thickly spread.
Cucumber peeled and sliced of course
So that we can tuck in hungry like a horse.
Scones with strawberry jam and cream
It is my idea of fulfilling a special dream.
Satiated, no room for sponge or fruit cake
Thank you Lord for all those that bake.

FRINTON ON SEA

To have a holiday there was my real intent
When a colleague of my husband went
Away on holiday and left his very nice home
Free for our family to live and roam.
The beds were made, rooms all neat and clean
Nothing out of place to be seen
My five young offspring were first instructed
All must be left and not destructed.
They went everyday to the nearby beach and ran
Into a hut, again so spick and span
I decided straight away, come what may, a big sigh
It would survive the onslaught of a fry.

This was made our home for the week to eat
Shelter when raining and wash our feet
Wet swimwear full of sand, buckets and spades
Shells and crabs here, with no maids
Would remain well away from the immaculate home
On their return the owners could comb.
Would find no evidence of cake crumbs on seats
Or carpets trodden with dirty feet.
Only a home smelling sweetly of lavender
While I went home to recover!

MY SOLDIER

I often see him standing still
Looking far back to that hill
Where long, too long ago
He stood steadfast against the foe
Young, oh he was only young
But he could speak the tongue
Of his Indian sepoys and men
Into the midst of the battle when
He'd only just begun to live
And then he was expected to give
His life for a supposedly just cause.

Then there was a slight pause
Of shells being fired overhead
As they advanced and he led
The soldiers up the hill to fight
In the darkness before first light
In faraway Burma against the Japs
Alert, not deceived by the lapse
Approaching the enemy's position
They prepared with ammunition
To retake the strategic post
Which their platoon needed most
When suddenly a shell burst
Amidst them and did its worst.

A piece of shrapnel hit his head
But far from being dead
He continued on to make a stand
Determined to hold this land
Until he was relieved of his position
Having achieved his mission
He was led away by the arm
So he would suffer no more harm
To a casualty clearing station
Into India awaiting evacuation.

There he first met nurses in grey
The QAs he remembers today.
There medics operated on his skull
And following a very brief lull
Into the thick of battle again
He was adamant even with pain.
The powers to be gave a military cross
Without him Pear Hill would be a loss.
That was the first of his awards
Four medals presented as rewards
For a life of military devotion
In Malaya, Borneo across the ocean.

Now I see him sitting in his chair
Nearly ninety years with thinning hair
Using energy looking after his wife
Caring for the rest of his life.

ON JOINING THE QAS

Starting nursing straight from school
Seven years later I thought I knew it all!
Rising from student to Staff Nurse and Sister
Calling all the consultants Sir and Mister
I expected to remain until I was Matron
With frilly lace cap and cuffs but no apron
One patient was a retired army major
And it was difficult to resist a wager
When he dared me to join the army
Remaining in the same place, I'd go barmy.
I should spread my wings and travel a bit
There would be uniform to wear and kit.

I applied and travelled to London Millbank
Where I was interviewed, my heart sank
There opposite me were four queen bees
I experienced some very weak knees.
I'd applied for a short service commission
For two years, they asked my permission
After consideration, if I would change it to four
Years if I was going to join the nursing corps.
That was after I replied, 'To the Far East'
Four years to go so far were the least
I could enlist for, so I agreed to amend
With fingers crossed they would send
Me, on joining, over eight thousand miles
And not forget me amongst the files.

The next stage in my interview
Expecting a medical, I had not a clue
That it was all a bit unsightly
Two brigadiers retired, but sprightly
Told me to take off first my shirt
Then bra, tights and skirt.
They told me to jump up and down
Well did they take me for a clown?
I was concerned these ex RAMC
Had overstepped the mark to see
Me in such disarray and was the test
To really see me at my best?
In their dotage their BPs could go high
I didn't wish to see them die.
At the end of the day if the other four
Applicants had to jump on the floor
Would these old fossils be in a state
When they returned to their wives, late?
They saw enough and clapped their hands
Declared me fit for far-off lands.

After basic training and a first post
I was en route to the place I wished to go most,
Out eastwards by plane, a very long flight
But where we really landed it wasn't quite
Expected, instead of HK it was Singapore
When the heat hit us after they opened the door
It was like putting one's head into an oven

We were told to be quick and not be sloven.
Met by a smart sergeant in a Land Rover
Who gave us more than the once over
After twenty four hours in the air
We were all bedraggled and beyond a care.
She eventually drove us to the officers' mess
After a detour but we couldn't care less.

Issued with tropical kit and sent to the ward
To roll up our sleeves, no time to be bored
We waited for weeks for a troop ship
Before embarking on a long nauseous trip.
We waited on the quayside before going on board
Where a group of sappers with one accord
Came over to say, 'Oh this will be fun'
As we lay on the deck catching the sun.
But the South China Sea had another idea
There was to be no frolics no fear,
As the wind increased to a typhoon
There was no dallying under the moon.
Marooned in our cabins for four long days
Counting chickens in advance never pays.
We lay moaning and groaning, seasick
Those young engineers, of nurses, had no pick.

Arriving early morning into HK harbour
Through the mist, new sights to savour
The Peak, on the island, rising high

Clouds descending, it reached to the sky.
There at the top was the military hospital.
The CBF's launch arrived alongside, with a call
'I've come to take you across to your transport'
Down the ladder, never fear you'll be caught
By the ensign in his smart bell bottoms of navy
We wondered why we had joined the army?
The transport was an open Jeep
And so we descended up the Peak
To our new place of work and play
I loved it all, No regrets to this day!

UPSTAIRS, OR IS IT DOWN?

The house was rambling across the ground
Where monks had trod and chants did sound.
The walls absorbing over the centuries long
The Gregorian hymns and the plainsong
If you are quiet and listen to the silence there
You will feel their presence nearly everywhere.
A small echo resounding around the walls
Sometimes waking me with their prayer calls.
It was an old priory in three distinct styles
Some may see it as ugly huge grey stone piles
But for me it was home, a place of grandeur
Rather worn, frayed and faded, but of wonder.
We were not affluent and landed county gentry
One of the hunting and shooting, assets a plenty
But simple country folk who happened to dwell
Above stairs and not below in a confined cell.
Did that give me a mixed up dual personality
Or has it enabled me to range high in society?
Never feeling inferior to the upper echelon rich,
Just as happy to nurse those found in a ditch.
To attend Garden Parties and meet those that give
Grand functions and enjoy how the other half live.

GOLDFINCHES

I can see they have appeared high in the beech tree,
One was on a recce ahead of the charm, to see
If the niger seeds, sunflowers, teasels are here
In feeders hanging from a tall oak table where
They expect to feed first, amongst other things.
Their white breasts, black with yellow-tipped wings
Are overshadowed by the red patch on their face
With their long slender beaks they try to keep pace
With starlings and sparrows who look absurd
Trying to compete with a more agile, delicate bird.
A charm or group of seven is usual, but I've seen
Two and three charms together, that have been
A flash of yellow, all swiftly darting together
They will even remain with a change in the weather.

A ROMANY HOLIDAY

Even in the seventies it was not easy to escape the noise
Of daily living, the roar of traffic and numerous toys.
So in our wisdom we decided to break away from tradition
And take the children on holiday to find on a mission
A return to nature's way of gentle living and experiencing
The countryside far away from the crowds celebrating
Sitting on beaches in the sun. We were going to have fun!
Hoping our five offspring would enjoy a good run.

In the Norfolk county there were some caravans for hire
They were of Romany origin and not ready to expire
With a domed rooftop of tin it looked rather sprite
A small painted wagon with bunks to flop on at night
Its wooden wheels polished and ready for the road
But what was going to pull this great heavy load?
We were introduced to Splasher, a white and brown steed
Which would obey our commands with the reins to lead
Him down off beaten tracks along grassy hedged verges
In the long lanes with wide open skies where land merges.
Staying at a trout farm with spring water to fill our pail
Clear, cool, fresh and sparkling, nature's perfect ale.
Going to bed with the sun as it slowly disappeared
Awakening at dawn, very early as a new day neared.

The minutes drifting into hours, no need to hurry
Just amble along at a slow pace with no scurry.

Listen to the buzzing bees, hear a rabbit sneeze
Was that a weasel or a stoat? See its prey freeze.
Fresh farm eggs from a gamekeeper on his way
To feed his pheasants at the start of his day.

There is so much to see, we decide there to stop
On a common outside a village with a shop
Where we could buy baked beans and bread
Having stopped the milkman for a fresh pint
As he wound his way round cottages of flint.

A windmill with its sails catching the east wind
Another experience for our young family to find.
Going along a road we were followed by a car
The driver stopped and asked us, 'Are you going far?'
He said he was a painter of gypsy family camps
Not sure if we were Romanies or just tramps.
Asking where we were going to spend the night.
My husband drew himself up to his full height
And said, 'My good man, you have not got it right'.
I wished he'd pretended, the picture worth a sight,
If it had been painted with us in the firelight.

PROFILE

Fifty-three years next month in November
You would imagine my face he'd remember!
I recently had my thinning hair cut very short
To update my Facebook profile, I thought
A new photo might be a wise suggestion
With my iPad camera, came the question
Should I a photographer have booked!
'Oh! who is that?' when my husband looked
First at the result of the brand new image.
And he did not recognise my profile visage.
I know he's lost sight, on the left of one eye
But is his right one also saying goodbye?
But I've seen him reading newspaper print
Is he trying very hard, to give me a broad hint
That with the ageing process fast setting in
And I am no longer young, slender and thin
Time has come to grow my hair long for a bun,
Or he may look elsewhere for a bit of fun?
On the other hand, perhaps it's a big tease
He'd need more energy and lose his wheeze!

OUR SPIRITUAL JOURNEY

'We are not human beings on a spiritual journey but spiritual beings on a human journey' - - Pierre Teilhard de Chardin

With hours of doing nothing but think
There's plenty of time to sink
Into a feeling of melancholy
Which might be a folly
Time for reflection
Also recollection
Pondering about life
I've tried to be a good wife
Working hard most of the time
Seeking the truth, and to be sublime.
A friend we'd not seen for years
Visited and, sensing fears,
Said, 'This is one life
Only for strife
When your soul
During its human role
Experiences frustration

Of letting go of destination

Losing, especially all the control

A lesson for progression of your soul.

His soul recognised my soul

He honoured the light

And love so bright

Kindness within

Faith now given

It is within him too

No difference or few

Miles between our world

A Buddhist a Christian revealed.

Perhaps at the end the same destiny

Hands together in farewell! *Namaste*.

A VERY SPECIAL EXPERIENCE

In Our Ladies' Hospital, Ipoh, Perak, Malaya

Our first daughter arrived too quickly
In Malaya where the heat made you prickly.
It was in the middle of the tropical night
I gave the midwife a terrible fright
She was on duty alone and very busy
Worked herself up into a great tizzy,
When I told her I was ready to deliver
My waters had broken like a river.
I was told she'd only one pair of hands
She needed good fairies with wands.

This experience, for next time, bode ill
And worried my baby could be born still,
So for my third delivery I looked around
Found a local convent on lovely ground.
The Indian nuns were all midwives

And had brought into the world many lives.
The delivery date was accurate and true
And in their habits of white and veils of blue
It was the day of Our Lady so blessed
That is why they were in that way dressed.

Walking in twos and singing the psalms
Their hands concealed in the habit's arms,
Their voices like angels up above
Raised in praise and glorious love.
It was so peaceful and very tranquil
An atmosphere so very still, until
I felt very special with slight contractions
Had to do very little and only slight actions.
The Mother Superior delayed her flight
Going back to Singapore, to see the sight
Of my baby deliver, without much pain
And said, 'What a wonderful birth', again and again!

MARCHING IN AND OUT OF QUARTERS

Our first was a hiring on the Chinese border
No quarter available
So for six months, we lived in total disorder
It was down a rough track
With a green roof, dragons on each corner
A primitive kitchen
Two bathrooms, a loo but no sauna
But we had a gardener
Who grew strange vegetables to eat
There were marigolds in abundance
The aphids to beat.
A lovely young Amah
Who cleaned, washed and cooked
Rice dishes and others
Which tasted better than they looked.

We lived in eight different quarters
Seven in the Far East
Some big enough for more daughters
But I always had the task

To march in and take over a grotty house
Having marched out
Leaving everything with no trace of a mouse.
I got rid of rodents
Fleas by the score until my hands were raw.
The QMs seemed to know
That I would work hard, not leave one flaw.
I was supposed to be
The Colonel's Lady, but no batman for me
A good thing that as a student
I'd learnt how to scrub and know how to see
The cobwebs and stains
Smell the drains, unblock U-bends and sinks
Bleach lavatories white
And get rid of all the obnoxious stinks.
Why when everything was
Sparkling bright and fit for a queen
Did another posting
Come through, with a squalid quarter to clean?

MALAYA

It was not long after the Malayan emergency
And the Battalion deployed
To the Peninsula, to prevent insurgency
Problems in Borneo started
And we were moved to another quarter
In Perak, which is in the north
There I brought forth a beautiful daughter
In BMH Kamunting
It was fifty miles away through the jungle
And rubber plantations.

The young QA midwife made a bungle
She was out of her depth
On her own at midnight, with three in last stage
She told me to hang on
But I could not control the urge to engage
My baby's head coming
Who was born so quick and with such ease.
Will you notify my husband's Duty Officer,
So that he'll tell him please
When he comes on parade.
Then with any luck, come and see us today?
But the young subaltern forgot
He had much on his mind about work and play.
I lay in bed thinking it was an army wife's lot!

RANK CONSCIOUS

When you're young, very fit and lithe
One does not have to strive
To retain an hourglass figure,
No please, don't snigger
I was not always overweight
But often looked rather great.
I played a lot of singles tennis
No, not with my husband Denis.
He was up to professional standard
And to be really candid
He did not like me to win at all
And I could really hit the ball.

In the QAs I was quite a catch
For anyone wanting a match
And all who wanted a tennis game
Officers, NCOs, what's in a name?

One day after many a long set
Back and forth over the net
I was summoned to the CO
Me at attention, he demanded to know,
'Was that a corporal I saw you play
With on the tennis court today?'
I confessed it was, he was a good shot.

But I had broken the rules, I was not
Allowed to fraternise with ranks below
How fortunate that the CO didn't know
The night before we'd been to the cinema
Nearly caught by two majors, sitting two rows ahead.
Conscious of rank
We kept a low profile, down our seats sank.
At the end of the film whilst still dark
Out we scurried, it was a bit of a lark.
I could never swallow the 'us and them'
Even when called, many times, 'Mem Sahib',
I never wore my husband's rank
It's far too snobbish, to be quite frank!

OPERATING THEATRE

High upon the peak
Came all those to seek
Medical help in Hong Kong
And from far away in Sekkong.
Serving in HM Forces, the infantry
Gurkhas, Lancers, mounted cavalry
Fusiliers recruited in the north
Needing care they came forth
By ambulance, Land Rover and car
It must have seemed quite far
As they wended their way
From the border all day
Along winding roads, over the sea
By star ferry for a small fee.
Round all the corners up the hill
Until they arrived at the hospital

First naval then army nurses
There to ease their pain and curses.
Young troopers blown up in a tank
Seeing those burns my heart sank,
Another whose arm was torn away
A burst duodenal ulcer, all in one day.
Amidst the routine cases on the list
Hernias,circumcisions and a wrist.

All young men, fit and strong
Before fate had served them wrong.

We were there to put them right
Repair the damage even at night.
On call twenty-four seven, to lend a hand
To the surgeon as we manned
The operating theatre on the top floor
Queen Alexandra's Royal Army Nursing Corps.

MOUNT KELLETT BRITISH MILITARY HOSPITAL

High on the Hong Kong peak
An imposing building for all to seek
Needing medical help with a pill,
Soldiers who were very ill
They also came who needed an op
In the theatre at the top
Of BMH Mount Kellett, where
A young nursing sister there
Would wait and prepare
To assist the surgeon with care.

One day it was quiet, no op to assist
Came a request she could not resist
The CO instructed her to go,
When the staffing was low,
Down to the officers' ward
Where she would not be bored.
There three MOs kept her talking
Down the corridor came walking
A good looking chap, finding the shirkers
The duty officer from the Gurkhas.

She did not see his rank
And her heart nearly sank
When she saw the MO frown
He outranked her with a crown
She quickly called him 'Sir'
And escorted him to where
The patient he had come to see.
But luckily he'd seen me!
It may have been the grey dress
Or calling him 'Sir' to impress.

He returned another day
All fifty miles, a long way
To the ferry, but first by train
To see me again and again!
It was the month of May
We fell in love. They say
'It was a whirlwind romance'
But it is not by any chance
That we are still together and not apart
After fifty three years it's still of the heart.

FUTURE?

As I lie still here and wait
There's time to contemplate
The changes in life
And the strife
I must accept
Learn to adapt
Not being so active
Learning to live
For each day
And enjoy if I may
The changes that arrive
At least I'm still alive
To see each morning anew
With the frost and the dew
Sparkling like stars in the sky
On rose petals, not high
They sparkle and shine
A day set to be fine
A chill in the air
To be fair
Autumn is here.
This time next year
Who knows where I'll be?
We'll just have to wait and see.

CLEAR SKIES

There is a crisp start
As the curtains pull apart,
Vapour trails flying high
Marking the clear blue sky
So many lines today
Criss-crossing in play
Noughts and crosses
Some winners, some losses.
Leaves are brown in patches
No longer matches
The green of the rest
But nature knows best.
With the advent of frost
We will find to our cost
The branches all bare
Our gardeners will care
When they sweep up the piles
Which go on for miles
Covering the lawn and beds
Hiding flower heads.
Then I must remember
We're nearing October
So when I'm exposed
The curtains must be closed.
With the bare tree
All will be free to see
Me, from the house behind
Not a pretty sight to find!

INVESTIGATION

I quietly open the door
Something falls on the floor
I'm glad it's not the peas
And my eye only sees
Chaos amidst the ice
Which I'll amend in a trice
The veg from the meat
But first on my seat
I'll need the top drawer
Before I tackle more.
Now I can reach all
Must not let it fall
I like everything in order
At the moment disorder
So set to, to sort
Oh! That was just caught
An ice-cream choc bar
But it did not go far.
I'll just move the fish
Into a clean dish
There's a beef pie
Now when did I buy
That, was it a year?
And do I need to fear
Salmonella or other

Bugs lurking?
Oh Bother!
There goes a roll
I'll need a long pole
With a claw on the end
Because I can't bend
But the rolls too hard
And I'm not on my guard
There goes a chip
Oh! How did that slip
Out of its bag?
I'm beginning to sag,
Back to my bed
And wait to be fed.

DISTRICT NURSING

How it's changed in my life,
I commuted without strife
But fresh for each day
To work hard with small pay.
We shared the workload
Kept to the nursing code.
When patients were sent home
And weren't free to roam
We ensured they had care
And wounds weren't left bare
But dressed when needed
My advice well heeded.
If a patient needed nursing
It was no good cursing
I got in my car
And not caring how far
Removed sutures or cast
Or my job wouldn't last.

Gone were the days
When through the byways
A nurse on a bike
Saved you the hike
She came to your abode
And heard you offload

All your aches and your pain
You would see her again.
You were one of her flock
Easy to spot in her navy blue frock.
In the sanctity of your home
Supported by nurses, you weren't alone
You felt safe and not threatened
When your health had weakened.
The nurse worked long hours
Never abused her powers
Of knowing your intimate detail
When limbs and organs fail
She became your friend
Often with you until the end.

Now it's called progression
But in reality regression
It's now come to the clinic
Even in your panic
They rarely visit your home
As a patient you go it alone.
Unless you have the big C
Macmillan comes without fee,
Which is small consolation,
When feelings are desolation
In any other severe illness
When needs are far less

Or so they decide
In the office where they hide.
They use a smart mobile phone
From their comfortable throne.
Their caseloads are small
They don't know their patients at all.
It was good in my day
And come what may
I am glad I got up at night
To tend to my flock in their plight.

GRASSHOPPER

The day was dull with cloud overhead
As I lay quietly on my bed.
The sun tried to appear once or twice
I thought for a while that all would be nice
I might lie here and dream
And think of strawberries and cream
The seasons over but for those grown indoors
Which never taste as ones with their flaws
Grown amidst straw set high on a bale
Come all weathers, sun, rain and hail.

Then out of my reach the unknown
Appeared, had something been blown?
But no wind stirs the tree or shrub
And yet on the window pane, a grub.
Looking closer, I was amazed
To see a grasshopper, rather dazed.
Not very big, about one inch long
Out of place - was something wrong?
Its strong hind femurs, antennae erect
Walking up and down trying to inspect
The white orchid residing on my sill
Alas the wrong side of the glass until
Suddenly it's gone like a catapult
Like an Olympic jumper without a fault.
Will it now begin to devour with an appetite
My precious new plants which give me delight?

AUTUMN

A season of change creeping in slowly but surely,
Nights are longer, the sun fading in the west early
Awakening those in far Japan and Hong Kong
And stays, to welcome their day, when before long
It's time to open the curtain and see its first ray
On a cooler morning at the start of our day.

A day sometimes with mist swirling
Like smoke from chimneys upwards curling
As they will before long as the fire in the grate
Begins to smoulder and then before too late
Bursts into flames and soon warms the room
So its cosy and snug like the place in a womb.

The leaves on the trees are beginning to turn
A soft yellow, red and brown as if a burn
Is singeing their edges and drying them
Slowly releasing stalk from the stem
Before they break free and float down
To cover the ground recently mown
Turf's last cut but now left until spring
The daisies asleep until again they will bring
Their sweet yellow faces and white hair
When the sun will return and the weather set fair.

THOUGHTS

Thoughts are so powerful we should be selective
When we convey them, to be really effective
In what we wish to portray
We need to be careful in what we think and say.
Is it mind over matter or matter over mind?
I am searching to decide or find
The answers to the strength of my thinking
Which dictates if I'm rising or sinking
I need to stay focused in my head
And try to overcome wanting to remain in bed.

It's safe within the confines of a bedroom
Under a duvet more like a womb
Where I cannot see if chaos reigns
In the kitchen where there may be blocked drains
Or on the oven shelves a baking tray
Where a pie needs disposing without delay.
Bananas in the freezer residing
And with fish pies are nearly colliding.

Ice creams have found a home in the 'fridge
Stacked up neatly to form a bridge
Of slowly melting pools of cream.
It's easier to remain here and dream
That everything is tidy and neat

Long curtains are opened with a pleat
Cushions in the chairs are plumped up
And there is nothing left curdling in a cup.
The carpets are not covered in drips
Where tea is spilled before reaching lips,
If only mugs were carried on a tray
I can only lie here and pray
That without delay I can resume control
And be back on patrol
To see that everything is in its place
And prevent me becoming a head case.

A PUZZLE

There is a question in my mind
The answer too evasive to find,
I glimpsed eternity one night
Then thought I had insight
Into the great unknown abyss
Where nothing was amiss
Where dreams came true
And problems few
Enclosed in arms within a bed
Sweet nothings whispered,
Is this the beginning of the end?
Can I leave you, lifelong friend?
Is it nearly time to go?
I wish now, not quite so slow
I want the end to come quick
But it is not for me to pick
For my soul to depart this place
I must await with good grace.

NEW TO MEDICINE

Two young ladies in their final year
Years of study and exams so near
Which will dictate where their future lies
Finding the lows and seeking the highs,
Will they follow medicine, surgery or GPs
Investigate conditions and disease?
Their aim to cure the patients on the ward
For the long hours worked, we should applaud.

They came to visit me today
Listened carefully when I had my say
Of when my troubles all occurred
Fresh in my mind, never blurred
By time, of that fateful day
Which cut short my work and play.
When a nerve block put in my tum
Dictated how I would walk or run.
For the remainder of my life
No longer a useful wife
Not free to bake and cook
No longer worth a second look.
But free to impart my thought
About what life to me has brought
The way medics failed with me to talk
And passed my bed would quickly walk

Without a second glance
In case I caught their eye by chance
And they would then have to explain
Why I had no movement or pain
In both my legs and right arm
Could they say why I had come to harm?

To these two with a vocation
Please remember good communication.
And remember relationships are vital
As the symptoms and signs in total
To build up a strong rapport
When difficult, do not ignore
But take time to talk and to hear
What it is that patients fear.
Sometimes it's better to confirm
Then help them to come to terms
With the possible outcome
And if recovery there will be some.

Maybe it's the end of the road
And you may need to lighten their load
By being frank, honest and sincere
Tell them that their end is near.
If you can't cure don't think you've erred,
As long as you have really cared.

HAIR

My hair needs a good cut
A bit thin on the top but
The back has grown long
And certainly looks wrong
It's lost all its shape
No longer just to the nape.
I missed the last visit
From Liz to cut off a bit
I was stuck here in bed
So no chance for my head
Of white thinning hair
To be cut or made fair.
Not that I want to be blonde
No one would be conned
I'm too old to pretend
Too late to amend
The damages of life
Exciting years as a wife.
So today with the sun
I'm up for a run
In my reliable cart
As quick as a dart
Liz has arrived
I'll have a short back and sides
I've seen Dame Judi Dench

A fine-looking wench
With hair short and fine
Very like mine
Or what it could be
I'll ask Liz and see
If she'll cut off my locks
And hope no one mocks
This ancient Briton
Trying to look like a kitten
With an elfin style
Hair on the floor in a pile
Maybe some make up
Will help me look like a pup
False eyelashes to replace
Those lost in the race
Which were long and thick
But no! They'll take the mick.
I will try to act my age
Because I'm wise as a sage!

MARSH KING

Tall, majestic, chestnut coat and flowing mane

For a horse so regal, an appropriate name

Marsh King, oh gentle giant!

So steady, sure-footed and so reliant.

Each morning at first light

You came to collect me to gaze at your height

The rider looked down from upon your back

Picked me up and then off for a hack.

I sat high upon the pommel, being just a tiny tot

My father sitting well into the saddle and off for a trot.

Over heath and training area so wild

An adventure for a little child.

I've never forgotten those days long ago

When over grass and keeping low

We kept away from firing guns

And soldiers out for morning runs.

It was just before they went to war

To ride, to run perhaps no more.

TIGGY, A LONG-HAIRED GINGER CAT

My mistress was getting on a bit
If I caught a mouse she had a fit
When she was ninety-one
She told me, time to move on.
A stranger came to the door
As I wasn't wanted any more
On her arm she had a basket
It looked rather like a casket.
Was this going to be my fate?
Could I escape? Oh no! Too late,
I ran and hid among the chairs
She caught me by a clump of hair.
I was put into that wicker hamper
Before I could try to scamper.
Into a noisy automobile
Her hands upon the steering wheel
Until a house came into view
And then without too much ado,
The basket was lifted and I could see
Something which frightened me, and made me pee
But I was not scolded
Gently in her arms was folded

Taken into her home
My matted hair sorted with a comb
Now I have a silky coat
Here I'll remain if it comes to vote.
The food seems good here indoors
But why have I got butter on my paws?
They are rather glad that here I came
Stopped deer coming into their domain
The muntjac were coming every night
Eating roses as if their right.
After many years of feeling safe
Things were spoilt with this waif
In came this mangy kitten
From mites she'd been bitten,
They thought I needed a mate
Well that nearly sealed her fate.
After years of being here, how obscene
Did not they realise I'm a queen?
I was so peeved, plotted and planned
To get Amber well and truly banned,
I sat upon the window sill
And waited ready for the kill
As she comes in through the flap
She'll fall right into my trap.
I jumped, landing on all fours

My outstretched claws in my paws,
Ready to take revenge on this cat
But her eyelids did not even bat.
She did not seem to care
Now with her long silky hair.
I suppose I must accept her
With her plaintive miaow and purr.
And learn to live together as friends
And wait until my nine lives end.

SIMON, A LONG-HAIRED CAT

One day there were cases and boxes
All labels, seals and locks
Packed away pictures and books
Leaving empty shelves and hooks.
A large container was filled to the brim
It all began to look rather grim.
Then to my surprise it became my turn
And to my horror I began to learn
That I too would be put in a crate
I could only await my fate.
I was loaded onto a plane
Would I see my mistress again?
It was a journey through the night
A long and frightening flight,
To a land away from Oman
I'm told I won't come to harm.
The plane arrived in damp and wet
I was checked over by a vet
All was fine and very well
Now that I'd survived the hell
Of being loaded in the hold
Where it was really cold.
A car journey a few miles west
Took me to find who I love best

My handsome couple from Oman
Were there and all is calm
In my new and comfortable abode
I can boast to other cats in the road.

SNOWY, A HEARING DOG

I had a difficult start to life
Full of woe and strife
I was found in a bag
Which began to sag
In the water deep
But before I fell asleep
Kind people rescued me
Took me to a centre to see
If I could be trained
No longer chained
As a dog to help the profound
Who cannot hear a sound.

They liked the look I had
And said they would be glad
To give me a home and tuition
Until I reached fruition.
When I was ready to be lent
A message to Sarah was sent
For her to come and train
And with me remain
To see if we got along
Not do anything wrong.

The days passed fast
And our fate was cast.
To her home I was sent
Several years have been spent
In perfect companionship
I never give her the slip,
On our long exciting walk
Each morning, with no need to talk
We are together
In every kind of weather.

I sleep upstairs so her can wake
When the alarm does make
The sound to arise and shine
It's good to know she's mine.
We start the day to work
And play, I never shirk
When the doorbell rings
And other things
Make a noise
I leave my toys
Touch her with my paw
So she'll open up the door.
I am rewarded with treats
With a smile she greets
Me if she goes away
Not too often parted for a day.

They say I should retire
To play before I expire
I would miss her company
Her loving, her empathy
She has never worked me
More than I should be
My maroon coat will be taken
But I will still awaken
Her with my paw on her bed
And I will then be fed.
I don't know how to shirk
As it's for love, not work.

BETTY

I am Betty, a hetty
My plumage is speckled
Black and white freckled
I've tried many a time
To safeguard my line
Hidden under hedges
And wheelbarrow ledges
The eggs I have laid
But the brood not made
The searches with torch
From back gate to porch
Every time find my clutch
Well away from the hutch.
I've learnt how to fly
Not far, but I try
My wings have been clipped
Day after day I have slipped
Out of the run

I try to have fun
I huff and I puff and give a big push
Out come my eggs under a bush.
I counted to four and then lost the score
Sitting clucking and brooding
Along came intruding
A push to one side
Exposed my backside and all was forsaken
The eggs were retrieved to have with their bacon
Am I never to have those chicks I adore?
never again to explore? I implore.

FEATHERED FEELINGS

I am Louis, a fertilising fowl
On holiday in a heaven for hens
So many in adjoining pens
Clucking and cackling, they left me in awe
Then over the wire in a flutter she soared
A speckled specimen in black and white
With her orange eyes a beautiful sight
Her ruffled plumage bright and clean
Beautiful Betty, best hen ever seen
To begin with I made a few cackles
Tried to fluff out my hackles
With the rush of blood to my head
My comb turned a bright red
I fluttered my wings
And a few other things
I knew what to do
And gave a loud crow
Betty followed me into my straw strewn nest
You can imagine the rest!

All went well and Betty, content
Waited a while then laid a few eggs
Hidden in my straw nest
Away from the rest
She thought they were safe well out of sight
She returned to the hen house
To be locked in for the night

Heads were counted, one was missing
Not my Betty, no wasted wishing.

So I, Louis, in my solitary confinement
Being a modern rooster would look after the eggs
To my surprise found a brown hen who begs
Me to leave her in situ covering the nest
And after today I need a good rest.
Then into the nest
Hands got hold of my guest
Took Brownie's two feet
She was well off her seat
Put her in with the hens
Secured tightly their pens
Then back came the boss
For the eggs, what a loss
I was left in the dark
Having made my mark
I'd done my duty
But we'd lost the booty

What a day of surprises
Delights and abuses
I'll try and squeeze through the hatch
From females no match
I'll beat a hasty retreat
Before they decide I'm good meat,

HENNY PENNY

I am Julie, a little brown hen
Much as I try
To escape from the pen
I am caught high and dry
Returned to the rest
Who lead a dull life
Staying close to the nest
It's me who's caused strife
Betty's my rival, a black and white bird
Has her eye on Louis, truly absurd
I'm not keen on men
Preferring the hen
It's her eggs I'm after
So far it's a disaster
To be a surrogate mother
They belong to another.

I'll try once again
To make my claim
I've found a pile under a tree
A strange colour, but we shall see
If I'm left long enough
Lie low in the rough
If them I can hatch
They may not match

Along comes the boss
Who seems rather cross
You're a hen that's so dumb!
Don't you know they're a plum?

COMPETITION FOR A COCKEREL

I thought he was mine and mine alone
And I'm not one to moan
About sharing the scratchings and grain
With those birds of little brain
But when Louis came to stay
It was only me that showed him how to play
How to help me build a nest
Far away from all the rest.
I showed him what to do
All this was very new,
His father kept him free from knowing
What every son should find when growing
That hens lay eggs which need a cover
From a feathered speckled lover.

He was my dream, my delight
In his pad at dead of night.
Then that was stopped by her indoors
I needed to sharpen up my claws
Young Julie started fluffing up her feathers

Sitting on my eggs, never mind the weather,
Trying to take over my cock
But did we both get quite a shock
When Louis found his way into our pen
And I do believe he fancied yet another hen.
How dare he show another nine
What I considered was only mine?
They all thought that he was theirs to share
When I had shown him what to do, unfair!
My speckled plumage matches his
Although our beaks are not made to kiss
And his offspring I may never know
But all those nights of bliss, oh! Wow!

MY HAREM

I am no longer banished to my den
But can roam freely like a hen
Instead of lonely nights
I can indulge in all my rights
With white, brown and speckled mates
I have never had so many dates
They bow and scratch around my feet
Until our feathers chance to meet.

Betty does not like it
No, not one little bit
But I'm just a male and very weak,
When I come across a beak
Which points in my direction
No time for inspection
Whether it belongs to black and white
Mount quickly, before she has a fright.

It's been a busy stay
In this harem far away
From my usual pecking run
Where my father has the fun
And rules the roost and keeps me
Far from being free
To enjoy a little light relief
Is my right, is my belief.

I had to wait until I came here
To indulge without fear
The pleasures of the night
Actually day as well, quite right!
I abandoned and escaped my pad
Eleven hens are now so glad
I found my way through their door
Do not go home yet, they implore.

A REAL GEM!

When you have a Gem
A dog not a hen
Then you can expect a cuddle
And at least a slight muddle
When you turn your back
She's on the attack
Don't leave your specs
If you don't want wrecks
Of Joseph Conrad design
You might hear her whine
She bites off its arm not knowing the harm
That a one sided frame
Makes it impossible to claim
That it's good for your image

And alters your visage
A trip to Specsavers
Where you ask a few favours
They produce a new arm
Leave your purse without harm
One new and one old side
'They suit you', they lied
Perhaps a new frame
Is the answer they claim
If you bought new lenses.
Could see which was the men's
If you went the whole hog, remembering this blog
Kept an eye on the dog!

SHARING EMOTIONAL PAIN

From across a wide sea
The pain was felt with a plea
Something which had started
Her father had sadly departed
The search for sister and brother
Queries unanswered from her mother
I have years of experience for sharing
For limb splinting and patient caring
And applying dressings to many a wound
But deep emotional hurts I have found
Too difficult and I cannot make right
Although I have tried with such might
To ease the pain in a young heart
Seeking the truth on her part
For far too many years
With unnecessary tears.
She's flown a long way
Across the Atlantic, a day
Tangible is the hurt I feel

When all I want is to appeal
To rectify and cure a deep hurt
When a reply by its absence is curt.
The hurt inflicted is not mine directly
But close enough to feel it irrespectively.
Several months ago I wrote a very long letter
To the person who needed to make things better.
I asked her to consider her actions and repair
The hurt inflicted on the innocent girl and care
For those tender in years who need her love
And to show them that she values above
All others that she is their true friend
In all words, deeds right to the end.
I waited in vain for that reply
But she continues to deny
And cannot bear to face
Admit, close the case.

THE MOON IS BRIGHT TONIGHT

Just above the clouds, but still very high
A huge disc of gold sails across the sky.
It was behind the beech tree
And I could see it looking at me,
Peeping through the remaining foliage
For a short time caught in a cage
Of leaves, or so it appeared
But it was moving swiftly as it peered
On its journey through the night
But for a short time a glorious sight.
I wanted the house to be on a pivot
So I could travel round with it
To follow and be bathed in its light
Throughout the neverending night

CLOSED DOORS

Confined to my bedroom like a naughty child
To say I feel cross is to put it mild
When my door is closed firmly or even ajar
I feel isolated, excluded and that a bar
Has been erected, which I find very hard
Because it makes me feel I have been barred.
I know this is not true, it's all in my mind
Because my husband and carers are kind.
It must be claustrophobia to feel enclosed
Or is it because I prefer to be exposed?
Not to the elements, there's a chill in the air
But to be part of our home's care and share
The decisions that keeps the wheels turning
And prevent the meals from burning.
To remain in solitarily confinement
Is not my idea of excitement
I like to be part of the place
Then you'll find a smile on my face!

RED NAILS

Being an old-fashioned nurse
Varnish was an unnecessary curse
After the night dressed for the town
Dolled up and our spirits to drown.
Back late and too tired to care
If the nails were not wiped bare.
Arriving on the ward next day
With varnish on and all hell to pay.
Sneak to the cupboard for acetone
The bottle empty and you are alone
With ten nails painted in bright red
If Sister found out you would be dead.
On female surgical with a patient conspire
Who has a full locker and remover acquire.
By removing the evidence of paint
You can regain the image of a saint!

A LITTLE KNOWLEDGE

Ignorance really is blissful and calm
You can bury your head in the sand
Pretend nothing is causing any harm
And not see further than your hand.
When signs are evident and you know
What they signify and be very aware
It's impossible to go with the flow
If it reflects on the future of care
For someone you hold very dear
I am prepared to fight to the end
So that investigations are clear
If it's possible to treat and mend
Then I will ensure the procedures
Are correct and provided unless
It causes him pain, is in vain and
Chemotherapy has nothing to gain.

FIGHTING HIS LAST BATTLE

A Leo by birth and by nature
Strong and courageous as always
Facing his last adventure
Head on, no hiding from the last days.
How many left is unknown
He may not want to let go of life
The seeds have been sown
The saying 'au revoir' to his wife
Will come when it's right
But now as he begins to discover
What it is he must fight
Investigations are yet to uncover
The reason for the sign
That not all is functioning well
The concern is more mine
I've seen it before and can tell.
At the age of many years
It is wrong to hold him back here
If suffering brings tears
However great my own fear
Of being too far behind
We always wanted to leave
Together and to find
Eternity, as we truly believe
I am his soul mate
He is mine which will
Dictate our fate

MY SENTRY

Hearing a cough in the night
I am alert, is he all right?
Is it just a tickle in the throat
Or has he lain too long and is about
To develop a deep vein thrombosis?
Or is this in my mind a deep neurosis?
I lie still with one ear open to sound
Is he sleeping now and has found
Peace from anxieties in his dream?
Lavish feasts with meringue and cream
Always a very sweet tooth for more
Fruit in abundance, even an apple core
Not too keen on broccoli but ate plenty
For forty years and left his plate empty
Before he told me what he thought
So I could then for the next years resort
To substitute and leave him content
As I never suspected and he's such a gent.

His dreams were more exciting in the past
Memories so vivid and they still last
He relives going on night patrol in the jungle
Searching for bandits, trying not to bungle
A mission to round up each dacoit in the way
Before his battalion can call it a day.
He is still light on his feet and moves with ease

Around the house, only given away by a sneeze
Being high tone deaf he can't hear the bell
Which I've attached to his keys so I know well
When he's wandering around in the dark
I need a dog which will stand guard and bark.
He is still trying to protect and watch over me
From those concerns he needs to be free,
To finish his journey with peace in his heart
And to know we won't be too long apart.

APPS

I have time to dream, to plan and waste
Doodling on my iPad there is no haste
But it would be very useful if my mind
Was as a young child to help me to find
An app which I know must be there
Hidden in the store, I'm sure it's not rare
I seek a Sasco planner, not for my wall
But to have on my screen and to call
Up the information about who views
My rear this morning, but no queues.
I found one to install and it was free
And thought the very answer for me.
The first appeared right but was lost
The second, again I'm glad at no cost
Display came up but not quite right
So in despair I resorted in my plight
To use what I had used years before
Modern technology and gadgets galore
Turned the clock back and ordered pages
For my Filofax, which I've had for ages.
So I will know who is coming when
Morning and afternoon and then
Again but I must fill it in with a pen!

LITIGATION

Every time I look at the news
Somewhere there is a claim
Because in someone's views
They are in pain or there's a maim
Whatever it is all the same
Because of negligence
Or you were called a name
And it is common practice
Everyone's after something
A reward for an injury
Frequently for nothing
Solicitors' hands are rubbing
After all it's your due
The phone keeps ringing
Enticing you to sue
The crack in the road
Which made you trip
When busy with a code
And lost your grip

You were engrossed
Your mobile got broken
The insurance is not enough
And you hurt your back too
You need to get tough
The solicitor said sue
They will take a percentage
Which is why they persist
To obtain your consent.
The lamp post they insist
Was to blame, in the way
It caused you to fall
Another very bad day.
But it's your call!

BATTALION ORDERS

It was in a country church on the Chinese border
Everything arranged through Part One Order
In the army at Battalion level this is how
Arrangements are made to clearly show
That events will take place in a certain way
Especially when it is for a wedding day.

Everyone knows their role and place
And they will be able to identify a face
Whether as an usher, best man or groom
They will know where to sit or stand in the room
Regimental orders kept all informed of the routine
Which had to comply to the second on the scene
The bride would arrive exactly two minutes late
Not one second longer or minutes, as their first date.

She would arrive on the arm of the Battalion Colonel
At the church door where bridesmaids would enable
The long train of her dress to spread far and wide
To cover the aisle carpet as she marched to his side.
He at attention in uniform, in its scabbard his sword
Realised through endurance he had got his reward.
They met in the May, a ring in July and now November
The fourth, fifty-three years ago, a day to remember
But that proud chap at the altar cannot now recall
That day when they first met and he was ten feet tall
As she called him 'Sir' and looked into his eyes
They knew there would never be any goodbyes.

HONEYMOON

We hitched a lift on an RAF plane
Nothing to lose, everything to gain.
From Hong Kong to far Singapore
We could not desire or wish for more
At the very start of our honeymoon
We shared two nights in a hotel room
Then to Kai Tak airport to go away
As VIPs in a Britannia the next day.

Arriving later in the Malaysian heat
We needed a cold shower for a treat
Together in the station hotel room
We stayed an hour for a quick groom
Before boarding the overnight train
And found our berths, singles a pain
Arrived early morning in the city of KL
A taxi to hire and a drive for a spell
Where we could relax and begin

Weeks of indulging is no longer a sin
In the comfort of a luxury holiday home
And free to come and if we please roam
Owned by the Sultan of Kedah and run
By the Chinese servants, of a kind man
In the Cameron Highlands a beautiful spot
Where roses and strawberries grow a lot
Cooler up in the hills away from the heat
The profuse sweating we could defeat
And makes one cooler and desirable
Also extra curricular most enjoyable.

A month of blissful eating and drinking
It was time to return to HK and soldiering
But the Cathay Pacific air crew were unkind
When they refused an apple for me to find
I found that air sickness was worse than the sea
I could not believe that it was happening to me
Unless there was a very good reason for the feeling
And I in the future with a new figure would be dealing.